I can feel good right now

soothing and inspiring wisdom from
~ Doctor Fun and the Collective

A collection of positive affirmations and ditties inspired to make you feel better and make you feel good.

Everything in this world vibrates and when you feel good you vibrate on a higher level. Great things can happen. Health, Wealth, Inspiration and Wisdom is yours.

This book is written by the "Dr Fun collective" which is Tim McGinnis tuned in tapped in and inspired by his own higher powers. These are his (or their) words.

*This moment
is the only DESTINATION
you will ever reach.*
~dfc

I Can feel good right now

Dr. Fun

We plant a tree
for every book sold

Copyright ©2016 Tim McGinnis
All rights reserved

The right of Tim McGinnis to be identified as author of this work has been asserted by him in accordance with the Copyright, Designers and Patents Act, 1988.

No paragraph or illustration of this publication may be reproduced, copied or transmitted without written permission from the publisher in accordance with the provision of the Copyright Act 1956 (as amended).

Paperback
ISBN 978-8792632-77-7

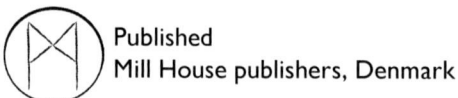
Published
Mill House publishers, Denmark

Disclaimer

The information contained in this book is intended to be educational and not for diagnosis, prescription or treatment of any kind of health disorder whatsoever. This information should not replace consultation with a competent health care professional. The content of this book may also be used as adjunct to a rational and responsible health care programme prescribed by a heatlh care practitioner. The author and publisher are in no way liable for any misuse of the material.

Contents

Introduction	vi
Better Feeling Story	3
Now	7
Ease and Flow	17
Abundance	33
On Creation	45
Source Energy	61
Energy lifter	73
Accept Yourself	75
Fun	103
Energy lifter	117
Expansion	119
Law of Attraction	137
Energy lifter	147
Mind	151
The Story of it All	165
About the author	173

My primary goal in this life journey is that of accepting myself EXACTLY as I am RIGHT NOW.

This often requires soothing the subtle undercurrent of
"improve this or improve that"
"stop this or stop that"
"do more of this or less of that"
"be more of this or less of that"

   Who I am today
   must be okay
   it really is
   the only way

~Dr. Fun

I can feel good right now

I Can Feel Good Right Now

CLARI-TEA

After after my morning cup of clari-tea
my life becomes so clear to me
That it's ME writing my story
and directing its scenes
as my inner-being guides me
showing me what it means
That I'm here to feel free
and I'm here to have fun
for adventure, love and expansion
all wrapped up in one.

~dfc

Better feeling story

Have you made the decision yet to commit yourself 100% to deliberately choosing to begin writing your new, amazing, powerful, invincible story?

The new story may feel forced at first. You may question if you're really sincere about it. You'll have good days and bad days. But, let me assure you my friend, once you decide to focus on one better feeling thought after another, moment by moment, hour by hour, day by day, you will surely begin to feel the momentum building.

You will feel yourself becoming more and more positive and confident that you really can be, or do, or have anything you want. You will begin to feel like the powerful creator you have always known yourself to be. You will even find yourself shrieking with delight from time to time at just how awesome YOU are!

When you march to the beat
of your very own drummer
each day's sure to feel
like the first day of summer

~dfc

I Can Feel Good Right Now

Finding a way to be HAPPY NOW Is the FASTEST way to start living HAPPILY EVER AFTER

6 ~ Dr Fun

Now

I aim to stay in this
............NOW
Yeah, that's the place
..........for ME
So I breathe and relax
clear my mind
.......Now I'm FREE!

~dfc

I Can Feel Good Right Now

this MOMENT
is the only place
that happiness
can ever
be found

And we can
find it NOW
by choosing
our object of FOCUS

~dfc

It's my job
and
my job only
to engender
my moment by moment
zenfulness
whatever it means
whatever it takes

~dfc

I Can Feel Good Right Now

Ya know,
I think I'll go ahead
and let this moment
be perfect
just
as
it
is.

~dfc

Every moment
is a
fresh
new
beginning

~dfc

I Can Feel Good Right Now

What I choose to focus on
in this moment
is the supreme decision
of my existence

~dfc

Surprise and Delight
Surprise and Delight
From morning til evening
and all through the night

~dfc

I Can Feel Good Right Now

    I slip from the grip
    of the details
    in this now
    and dissolve into the freedom
    from the way, the means, the how
    ~dFc

RIGHT NOW
seems like
the PERFECT time
to remember
that I have
COUNTLESS legions
of spiritual assistants
EAGER and AVAILABLE
to SUPPORT me
with ANYTHING
that CONCERNS me
RIGHT NOW

~dfc

I Can Feel Good Right Now

        I felt the EASE
        Then I felt the FLOW
        The energy started to
        MOVE
        Now all systems are GO

                    ~dFc

EASE AND FLOW

There's nothing you need to "give up" or "overcome" or "change" in order to be a more spiritually evolved person.

Simply breathe, allow, be easy and accept yourself as already perfect, loved and complete.

And the behaviors that don't add to your higher joy will fall away like the autumn leaves.

I Can Feel Good Right Now

just lay back
....relax.....
and let the river
do the work

~dfc

I decided to find my peace inside
no matter where I go
Whether I walk or drive or ride or skip,
or even if I row.

~dfc

I Can Feel Good Right Now

Today
I choose
to relax my expectations
of how I think
my life should be
so that
I may fully
accept my life
exactly as it is
...perfect!

~dfc

Calmly receive
the EASE
that gently flows
to you today.

~dFc

I Can Feel Good Right Now

The circumstances of your life
are PERFECTLY ALIGNED
with your reason for being here.

EVERYTHING
is
ALWAYS
just as it should be

~dfc

Here I am
with ME again
I breathe in deep
and look within.

I breathe out fully
releasing stress
allowing calm
on me to rest.
~dfc

I Can Feel Good Right Now

The unfolding
is perfect
Oh yes!
I've decided
So I chill
and stay still
and feel
utterly guided

~dfc

When experiencing an undesirable or uncomfortable situation, it might be interesting to pause a moment and ask,

"*How does my eternal, infinite, powerful, loving, all-knowing self view this situation?*"

Then pause to listen....

Pretty cool, right?

~dfc

I Can Feel Good Right Now

Listen, listen, listen
to the voice you have inside
for surely when you listen close
you'll have the sweetest ride

~dfc

A centering mantra:
Pause a moment,
Breathe,

"I am here
in this now
all of me
I allow"

~dFc

I Can Feel Good Right Now

Inhale.
Exhale.

I am willing and open
to allowing this moment
to be perfect.
just as it is.

Inhale.
Exhale.

And so it is.

~dFc

We can always know when we're flowing from our true self; it feels easy, light, natural and fun.

I Can Feel Good Right Now

I love flowing the flow
from my innermost being
It's so easy and light
and utterly freeing.

~dFc

Morning's first light,
sun peeks through mist on the horizon
sweet caress of knowing
dances gently over my skin
fills me with clarity
and peace within

~dFc

I Can Feel Good Right Now

Relax and allow
let all things just be
For it's with ease
the rain falls
then flows to the sea.

~dFc

Abundance

MONEY
Which one feels better?

"Earning and making money"
OR
"Attracting and allowing money"?

Earning and making money implies using the commonly agreed upon pay-scales, methods and work hours for different tasks that currently exist in our society.

A lawyer makes this much, a teacher that, an office worker that, and so on. Pick the one that fits your interests and training and you will know the kind of lifestyle you can expect.

Attracting and allowing money focuses on vibrational resonance, on the magic of the universe, on avenues of money never before heard of or imagined in the human experience.

This method can bring with it new and fresh ideas, unexpected rendezvous, fun, excitement, new people and new places.

But it's also more uncertain, riskier, adventurous.

I Can Feel Good Right Now

It takes practice, and a commitment to learning a new relationship with money and income.

Most people have chosen the former. I believe that most of you reading this message have chosen the latter, or at least you desire to.

It is my great desire to learn and become an expert in allowing and attracting money.

And desire is the most important ingredient.

What about you?

~dr.fun.collective

I can feel ABUNDANT
any time I CHOOSE.

~dFc

I Can Feel Good Right Now

Breathe in DEEPLY from WHEREVER you are in your life.....

It IS perfect, and abundance surrounds you.

I can see abundance
everywhere I look

~dfc

I Can Feel Good Right Now

Perfectly perfect
Divinely divine
All I desire
Comes perfectly timed

~dfc

There's an energy that's flowing to us
it's the energy that creates worlds
all day and all night Like a hose flowing water that makes a garden grow
All we have to do is
tend to the flow
tend to the flow
Keep our valves of allowing open
and our lives, in ABUNDANCE, will grow!

~dfc

I Can Feel Good Right Now

Every day
In every way
Streams of abundance
Flow my way

~dfc

Abundance is a feeling
that I can feel right now
It comes from how I feel inside
not from what I see around

~dfc

I Can Feel Good Right Now

In life we find our greatest wealth
as we learn to live from our highest self.

~dfc

I rest in the fullness
of all that rests in me

~dfc

I Can Feel Good Right Now

As I let it be easy
and simply unfold
new horizons reveal
stories yet to be told.

~dFc

ON CREATION

All thought comes in response to our vibration. We are not actually the "creator" of the thoughts we receive, but rather the receivers of already existing thought forms. When we deliberately focus on feeling good, we will receive thoughts to match.

Consistently holding this intention is at the heart of deliberate creation.

~dfc

One thought
One breath
One point of focus
at a time.
And your success is
guaranteed.

~dFc

I Can Feel Good Right Now

Clarity first,
then inspiration
It feels so good,
just like a vacation

From vibration,
to thought,
to action we go

It's the best place to be,
swept up in the FLOW.

~dfc

The best things in life
come easily

~dfc

I Can Feel Good Right Now

I love how SIMPLE and EASY it is
to just DO WHAT I LOVE
and then
WATCH the UNFOLDING

~dfc

My job is to do
what I do BEST
and let the Universe
take care of the rest

~dfc

I Can Feel Good Right Now

My expertise? My expert ease.

Reduction of effort = increase in output

~dfc

I Can Feel Good Right Now

If you want it
you can have it
It will come to you
at the perfect time
and in
the perfect way

If you don't have it yet
That's okay
It only means that
all of the necessary
components
are still lining up

For the perfect time
and
the perfect way
of it all

~dfc

I love the perfect timing
I love the ease and flow
I love to see the ducks line up
So neatly in a row

~dfc

I Can Feel Good Right Now

Your cake is baking
it smells delicious
it will be ready
when the timer goes off
then it will need some time to cool
then it will be frosted and perhaps decorated
Then the plates and cutlery will be set out
It will be sliced to perfection
Then some ice cream as well, perchance

It's time.
The first bite..
Oh my, it was worth the wait
Oh yes it was.

~dfc

I can let it be easy
I can let it just come
and reveal itself slowly
like the first light of sun

~dfc

I Can Feel Good Right Now

I'm trusting the rhythm
and feelin' the vibe
As the Heart Universal
beats perfectly timed.

~dfc

Magical rendezvous
fill my path
The more I let go
and let myself laugh.

~dfc

I Can Feel Good Right Now

Stay in your sweet spot..that light and fun place where you feel great, while sharing your truest essence...

Stay there, stay there, stay there

and the Universe will bring you the people who love doing the things that you don't....

and they will do those things from their sweet spot. Isn't that great to remember!?

~dFc

I pause to breathe into the awareness that all is well.
Everything is always working out for ME.
~dFc

I Can Feel Good Right Now

Are you doin' it "like a boss" today?

Like a boss today I woke up and I gave up
and I did it like a boss
I put my hands up and surrendered
and I did it like a boss
I decided I would let it all be easy
like a boss
Now I'm flowin' and I'm chillin'
and high vibin'
Like a boss

~dfc

Source Energy

My number one priority is maintaining my alignment with Source, or as I like to say it, "*Tending to my energy flow*" That means that what is happening "out there", whether, financially, relationally, health-wise, career, etc....is IRRELEVANT compared to the condition of my "energy flow".

As I am aligned with Source, I can feel the energy of Source flowing through me. I get inspired ideas, fun thoughts, helpful reminders, the feelings of love, passion, inspiration etc....and the more I stay aligned, the more I can feel the energy flow increase in intensity and consistency. So, as I go through my day, I'm constantly checking in with how my energy feels...and making adjustments from there.

It's a matter of where I'm directing my FOCUS. When I focus "out there", I will tend to mirror my feelings based on what I'm observing, but when I'm focused on my "energy flow" I know that I am in touch with the Source of everything. And that's the key to everything.

~Dr Fun Collective

I Can Feel Good Right Now

I breathe deep
and align
with my essence,
the Divine

To find my Inner-being alignment
Is my highest
Earth-assignment

~dfc

Clarity, clear,
clarity, clear,
unfolding,
beholding,
right now and here.

From deep within
or high above
the words of Source
always bring love.

~dfc

I Can Feel Good Right Now

My CONNECTION
with PERFECTION
is my natural
PREDILECTION .

~dfc

OBEY your ENERGY
This ENERGY flows to you
and through you
ALWAYS It flavors
your labors
And lights up your DAYS
It charges your cells
With passion and FIRE
And lights up your circuits
Of LOVE and DESIRE

~dfc

I Can Feel Good Right Now

When I focus on what's working
I amplify the vibe
Of all the things that make me smile
And make me feel alive

~dfc

I looked up in the sky today
And saw a boiling hot ball of flames
From 93 million miles away
It sent me its 10 thousand degree rays
that landed like butterflies on my skin.

~dfc

I Can Feel Good Right Now

Dialing into perfect flow
the ease of trees
the grass that grows
the sun that shines
bringing heat and light
I fall back in the arms
of this Universe of Delight

~dfc

Thank you for
the HERE
Thank you for
the NOW

I focus on the
What and Why
and give to Source
the HOW.

~dfc

I Can Feel Good Right Now

Clarity, focus, ease and flow
my inner-being guides me
Wherever I go

~dfc

I breathe in deep
I receive the FLOW
that brought me
to where I am
and guides me
to where I go

~dfc

Energy-Lifter

Everyday I'm finding more and more evidence to support the fact that:

I am a powerful creator.
I get more of what I focus on.
Everything I desire is because of how I will feel when I have it.
I am a lover to the very core of my being.
There's nothing better than feeling good unconditionally.
Everything is always working out for me.

The universe loves to surprise and delight me.
I can't get it wrong and I'll never get it done.
Everything is always working out for me.

The better it gets the better it gets.
MORE is the mantra of the universe.
This moment is all that exists.
I came here to experience joy.
Contrast is my friend.
Expansion feels amazing.
We're all in this together.
Everything's unfolding perfectly for me.

I Can Feel Good Right Now

My emotions are always telling me whether I'm agreeing with my inner-being's perspective or not.
I have the energy that creates worlds in my pocket and all times.
I am the creator of my reality.
I am the writer of my story.
Everything's unfolding perfectly for me.

Everything I desire will come to me when I find the vibration of it.
Feeling good now is the fastest way to living my dream life.
Having fun everyday IS doing the work of alignment.
Anytime I feel negative emotion, I know what to do to feel better.
My inner being is always guiding me on the best possible route to what I desire.
My inner-being knows where I am and knows where I want to be and is always guiding me step by step to get there.
All is well and getting better every moment of every day.

~dr Fun collective

ACCEPT YOURSELF

If you've ever wondered why it feels impossible to fix yourself......it's because you were never broken to begin with.

Read with conviction and full knowing:
My vibration is clear.
My intention is strong.
My knowing is boundless.
My spirit is vibrant.
I am eternal.
I am infinite.
I am love.
I am me.

~dFc

I Can Feel Good Right Now

Only ONE person needs to GET you....
and that person is YOU!!!
And if YOU don't GET YOU yet
don't worry
there's no hurry.
The fun is in the unfolding....

~dfc

Accept yourself EXACTLY where you are RIGHT NOW.

This includes:

your behavior, diet, career, relationships, emotional quirks, habits, financial situation, living situation, desires, propensities, education, perceived mental health, and everything else you can fit in here.

ACCEPT YOURSELF

Fully. Completely. Willingly. Gladly. Boldly. Bravely. Lovingly. Kindly. Magnanimously. Robustly. Proudly. Openly.

I'M NOT JOKING.

Because this is EXACTLY how the Source within you sees YOU. The Source within you NEVER has a list of things you need to CHANGE.

"But Dr. Fun....I thought that I came here to CHANGE and GROW?"

Good point. YES YOU DID....

From your POSITION of SELF-LOVE and ACCEPTANCE the Vortex Version of YOU will be FULLY allowed to organically and effortlessly UNFOLD in your experience.

That's right.

True change and evolution happens AFTER we are in the position of unconditional self-love and NEVER because we are aware of something wrong with us that NEEDS to CHANGE!

I Can Feel Good Right Now

Let me say this again....Source NEVER uses our perception of something NEEDING TO CHANGE as a reason to initiate change in us. Because SOURCE NEVER sees us as LACKING in ANY way!

In Summary, the ONLY way to CHANGE, EVOLVE, GROW, DEVELOP organically, is to ACCEPT YOURSELF JUST AS YOU ARE TODAY.

Can you feel how RADICAL this is?

It is the ANTITHESIS of the WORLD'S SYSTEM we have been taught and trained in....and it takes LOTS of PRACTICE

"Allowing. Accepting.

Now. Now. Now....

I am perfect just as I am....."

If you can say that with any degree of sincerity, you are truly ready for Source to work its magic through you.

~doctor.fun.collective.

It's All Okay

Okay.

I feel fat - okay
I feel thin - okay
I feel poor - okay
I feel rich - okay
I feel alone - okay
I feel loved - okay
I feel unhealthy - okay
I feel healthy - okay
I feel directionless - okay
I feel full of purpose - okay
I feel dumb - okay
I feel intelligent - okay
I feel frustrated - okay
I feel satisfied - okay
I feel short - okay
I feel tall - okay

I feel, I feel, I feel...
Okay, okay, okay...

It's ALL okay....just as it is...

~dfc

I Can Feel Good Right Now

There is nothing
"out there"
that I need
to complete me.
but rather
the ever-expanding
realization
that I already am.

~dfc

I am that which i seek.
 ~dFc

I Can Feel Good Right Now

Learning to be a DELIBERATE CREATOR takes a lot of practice, friends. It's a whole new way of thinking, living, and being.

So be nice to yourself.

You're doing the best you can.

Thank you.

~dr.fun.collective

What are commonly referred to as "mistakes"
are merely "clarity building opportunities"

Remember this: if it feels good IT'S TRUE.
Has it ever felt good to say "I made a mistake"?
Nope.
Because mistakes are an illusion...just like scarcity...

~dfc

I Can Feel Good Right Now

I'm a problem MAKER
a solution ALLOWER
When I realize this
I feel my VORTEX POWER

Oh what a boring world it would be
if everyone else agreed with me

~dfc

A young man contacted me recently in search of guidance and comfort for some pain and confusion over a relationship.

I wrote him the following:

> All is well
> You've got this
> Be easy about it
> There are no wrong choices.

These are essentially the words our inner-being is speaking to us all, day every day.

When we can't hear them, we reach out for the words of another person.

That's okay. We've been taught to seek the wisdom of others.

But it's wonderful to know that we each of us has direct access to the special wisdom coming from our higher self, always customized for us and always perfect for every situation and circumstance.

~dfc

I Can Feel Good Right Now

When the Tired Old Stories
come back to me
asking to be retold
a smile comes on my face
and with a consoling embrace,
I proclaim
"So sorry man, but you've been sold!"

~dfc

do you want MORE of it?
then,
by all means,
talk about it!

What we continue
to remember
we are bound
to repeat.

~dfc

I Can Feel Good Right Now

"This is how it happened before"
So I set it to the side
Then I pause a mo' and quiet my mind
and take a fresh, new ride

~dfc

Inhale
Exhale

Relax
Receive
Renewed
Believe.

~dfc

I Can Feel Good Right Now

I release and let go
of my Tired Old Story
I think it's time I let it sleep
I used to wake it everyday,
to come outside and play
But now I say,
"Forever Rest In Peace"

~dfc

I love KNOWING
that ALL I have lived
has made me who I AM
in this MOMENT

~dfc

I Can Feel Good Right Now

Can you SMELL it?
Take a MOMENT.
Breathe in DEEPLY.
Remember why you came here.
You came HERE to express yourself
in WAYS that only YOU can!
TODAY is a NEW DAY!
Anything is POSSIBLE!

~dfc

Better and better
More and more
That's what we all
came here for!

~dfc

I Can Feel Good Right Now

Speak to your soul:

[Inhale]
"I am perfect
just as I am
right now"
[Exhale]

x5

This truth is activated within you now

~dFc

I will mind my own Blissness.

I Can Feel Good Right Now

Habitual
self-restriction and monitoring
do NOT promote
a FREE and HAPPY life

Be self-generous
release the reins
feel the flow

~dfc

Embrace your "addictions" and speak tenderly to them.

It will give them the courage they need to live without you.

~dFc

I Can Feel Good Right Now

Nobody can offend, perturb, anger, vex, exasperate, deceive, hoodwink, irritate, respect, love, adore, cherish, appreciate me ...
without my vibrational permission.

~dfc

You DON'T need
to TRUST in anyone else.
Not in him
or her
or me.
Just find the trusting place
between YOU and YOU
and all others,
with you,
shall agree.

~dfc

I Can Feel Good Right Now

Flowing,
clearly flowing
from the place of deepest knowing
and all around me
love is growing
faces beaming,
spirits glowing

~ dfc

100 ~ Dr Fun

When I align
with the best of me
The beauty in others
is all I can see

~dfc

I Can Feel Good Right Now

Focus on feeling good.
Look for reasons to smile.
Look for reasons to laugh.
Look for reasons to appreciate.
Pamper myself.
Listen to myself.

Adore myself.
BE MYSELF!

~dfc

Fun

Fun
Fun
Passion
Desire
I'm livin' my life
like the roof is on fire

~dfc

I Can Feel Good Right Now

REVELation- the awareness that anytime is the right time for a party.

~dFc

Oh how I love the HELL YES!
The taste and touch and smell YES!
The thousand falling stars at night
and scent of all is well YES!!!

~dFC

I Can Feel Good Right Now

I'm flying high
I'm flying high
I passed the clouds
then kissed the sky
Skied down the craters on the moon
I skipped on stars while I sang a tune
I put cold water on the surface of Mars
then made some tea and ate candy bars
I dove into the center of the sun
Of course it was hot, but oh boy was it fun
I frolicked in rivers of molten delight
Of course only DOWNSTREAM
You know I got that part RIGHT!

~dfc

To believe in only what we can see,
Is living in the past
So let's drop our line
in the pool of Divine,
Where the living is a BLAST!

~ dFc

I Can Feel Good Right Now

Tuning into the station
of my highest delight
Where the fun hits are played
From morning til night
             ~dFc

Try less
Chill more
And the flow will sweep you off the floor
Think less
Laugh more
And joy will swoosh you out the door

~dFc

I Can Feel Good Right Now

I inhale appreciation
and I exhale bliss
How does it get
any better than this?

~dFc

110 ~ Dr Fun

It feels good to accept that I can't get it wrong and I'll never get it done, so I might as well have some fun, fun, fun!!
We ez dun!

dr.fun.collective

I Can Feel Good Right Now

Our only JOB is the Joy Of Being
~dFc

112 ~ Dr Fun

It's not really about losing weight or getting more money or finding the perfect lover, or, or, or...

It's ultimately about removing these criteria once and for all from our happiness equation.

It doesn't matter what you eat. It only matters how you feel when you eat it!

It doesn't matter what you think. It only matters how you feel when you think it!

It doesn't matter what you do. It only matters how you feel when you do it!

~dFc

I Can Feel Good Right Now

Around every corner
around every bend
adventures await me
and joys without end

~dfc

114 ~ Dr Fun

the fun
the fun
is never done

~dfc

I Can Feel Good Right Now

The FASTEST route to your DREAM LIFE, is to LOVE the life you have NOW.

~dFc

ENERGY-LIFTER

RIGHT NOW is the perfect time to:
Love myself completely.
Trust the clarity of my inner-guidance.
Accept the perfection of this moment.
Embrace the beauty of my body.
Adore the sharpness of my mind.
Appreciate the perfection of my timing.

Believe in the certainty of my worthiness.
Relax in the unfolding of my path.
Honor the value of my contrast.
Bask in the perfection of my knowing.

Delight in the intricacies of my desires.
Adore the beauty of my spirit.
Marvel at the complexity of my body.
Make fun an essential part of my day.
Breathe often and deeply.

Acknowledge the eternalness of my existence.
Magnify what's going well in my life and ignore what's not.
Talk more and more about things that feel good.

I Can Feel Good Right Now

EXPANSION

Most of us spend our lives trying to win approval from the very same people we chose to cause the most expansion in our lives.

What do you mean Dr. Fun?

Well, how do we expand? From contrast.

Who are the best people to give us contrast?

Our family members.

How do our family members give us contrast? By misunderstanding us, trying to form us into their view of what it means to be happy and successful, by trying to teach us to take the safe path, to avoid all danger and to be good little boys and girls..and all of this in the best way they knew how...(Yikes!!!)

And yet after we've launched massive rockets of expansion, we still long for them to finally give us the green light of approval before we'll allow ourselves to align with our expanded self..(that they helped create from the contrast)

Are you starting to see the humor?

Our families have already done their work by helping us to launch such amazing rockets of desire...Now let's LEAVE THEM OUT OF IT, and just ALIGN with our EXPANDED SELVES...

Are you getting it? I love the fact that my family doesn't

I Can Feel Good Right Now

"GET ME"! That's NOT their fleebin' job! I know that they LOVE me....but they don't GET ME....and I LOVE IT THAT WAY!

I didn't choose a family that would GET ME! Or even a SOCIETY for that matter.

Every time that someone doesn't GET ME, it forces ME to GET ME!

You get it..?

It's YOUR JOB TO GET YOU! NO ONE ELSE'S

Now you must be laughing by now....because this is jolly hilarious...how many years we've spent trying to get other people to UNDERSTAND US and SUPPORT US, and GET US!

> It's YOUR JOB....
> to...
> GET YOU..
> and NO ONE ELSE'S

> It's YOUR JOB...
> to LINE UP with your DESIRES...
> and NO ONE ELSE'S

> It's YOUR JOB...

to live in a way that makes
YOU HAPPY...
and NO ONE ELSE'S

ROFL! [rolling on the floor laughing]

Now, I know you're laughing...and crying tears of relief....
...because it's always been so eeassyyy..

NOTE:
If your family was and is super duper awesomely supportive, then substitute who or whatever has been responsible for most of your expansion.

~dfc

Vortexual focus:
The intentional summoning of my creative energies
in the direction of a specific topic
or general knowing,
that my SOURCE-self has already BECOME
and is CALLING me to ALIGN,
with the purpose of finding and maintaining
the VIBRATIONAL ESSENCE, or FEELING
of my expanded self.

"The THAT that makes me feel like THIS"
Oh how I wish I had THAT
So I could feel like THIS
Oh how I wish I had THAT
So I could feel like THIS
Oh how I wish I had THAT
So I could feel like THIS
Feel like THIS
Feel like THIS
Feel like THIS..... Oh, wow, I'm really starting to feel like THIS.
The THIS that I thought
that THAT would bring.
Now that I feel like THIS
I can relax and sing
And of course that THAT will come in perfect time
But I'm in no hurry since I'm feeling like THIS
And this THIS is a feeling so very FINE.

~dfc

I Can Feel Good Right Now

The feeling of "I want it now" is an indicator that we are still focused on the lack of what is wanted.

That's what makes the desire feel so acute.

And that's why things always come after we've chilled wayyyy out.

~dFc

The having
and then not having
and then having
and then not having
are what make up
the waves
of expansion

~dfc

I Can Feel Good Right Now

I have come here to take thought beyond what it has ever been before.

I have come to expand my consciousness and the consciousness of everyone I meet.

I have come to ask huge questions and receive huge answers.

I have come to learn the key to happiness, then joyfully and playfully share it with others.

I have come to receive thoughts from the greatest minds who have ever lived and present them in a way that makes people, laugh, cry, understand, live, grow, love, relax, dance, play and sing.

YOU?

Dr. Fun & the Collective

Contrast is our ever faithful friend, guiding us and goading us into the transformation of our indecision into clear and ardent desire.

~dFc

I Can Feel Good Right Now

Didn't find my groove today
Sometimes that's how it goes
It's all just perfect anyway
'Cause that's how Clarity grows

~dFc

Embrace your highs and your lows.
You can't have one without the other.

Without the illusion of separation,
we can't have that blessed feeling
of coming home.

~dFc

I Can Feel Good Right Now

Unwanted topics and beliefs die from lack of attention. Period. When we focus on something because we want to change it, we are actually making it stronger because of our attention to it.

The only way to change something "unwanted" is to go general and find any reason to feel good as often as possible for as long as possible.

~dFc

I'm swimming in perfection
Perfection all around
Perfection in the sky
Perfection on the ground
Perfection on the hills
and in the fields below
Perfection's all I choose to see
No matter where I go
                        ~dFc

I Can Feel Good Right Now

The absolute worst time to try and solve a problem is when we're really feeling that it NEEDS to be solved.

Our first order of business when we are facing a situation that feels like a problem, is to find a way to chill out, let it go and distract ourselves. Now the solution is on its way.

~dFc

I grabbed the ease from the cupboard
and the flow from the drawer
Mixed 'em up and drank 'em down
Now I'm groovin' out the door.

                                          ~dFc

I Can Feel Good Right Now

From where I am right now,

I welcome ALIGNMENT
I welcome PEACE
I welcome SERENITY
I welcome CALM
I welcome CLARITY
I welcome KNOWING
I welcome CONFIDENCE
I welcome POWER
I welcome PASSION
I welcome ENTHUSIASM
I welcome ENGAGEMENT
I welcome CONTRAST
I welcome EXPANSION
I welcome FLOW
I welcome EASE
I welcome ALLOWING
I welcome BOOM BOOM POWING

I welcome SMILES
I welcome LAUGHTER
I welcome GIGGLES
I welcome LIGHTNESS
I welcome AIRINESS
I welcome AWARENESS
I welcome CONFIDENCE
I welcome LOVE
I welcome ACCEPTANCE
I welcome BELIEF
I welcome STRENGTH
I welcome STABILITY
I welcome POSITIVE MOMENTUM
I welcome FULLNESS
I welcome ABUNDANCE
I welcome NEWNESS
I welcome ALL OF ME-NESS

~dfc

I Can Feel Good Right Now

To think that
I SHOULD be doing
something OTHER than
what I AM doing
is RESISTANCE
and is
counterproductive

NOW
is a fine time
to accept it ALL
as PERFECT

dr fun and the collective

The Law of Attraction

attract = to draw things to me.

There is nothing to "go and get"
"If you want it, go and get it!!"....nah

My frequency draws things to me.

Like a radio station draws the type of music corresponding to its frequency. Well, maybe "match" or "resonate" are better words, but you get the idea.

So there is country music flying through the air on the wings of 95.7 FM, rock music, at 91.1, classical music at 88.9, pop music @ 101.5, rap music at 96.3 and oldies at 94.1

You don't "go and get" the music; you tune to it. And you can't manipulate the radio waves to change their tune. They're all there, all the time, in the air, waiting to be tuned in to.

This is also true for the emotional/vibrational frequencies floating around us at all times. And we can know which "station" we're on by how we're feeling and what we're hearing.

It's all about adjusting our emotional dial,
finding ways to feel better
to relax and be easy about things..

This in essence, causes the adjusting of our vibrational dial. And although changing a radio dial is quite effortless, changing our emotional frequency takes practice.

I Can Feel Good Right Now

Moment by moment modulation

For me, the most powerful realization is knowing that it's up to ME to change the dial, and I CAN DO IT!!!

That puts all the power in my hands....

And as always, the easiest way to change the dial is to let go of the reins, chill out, stop "trying" so hard to make things happen..essentially, to focus all my attention on feeling good inside of ME, and leaving everything and everyone else out of it...

It's really a lot of fun.

~dfc

All I desire is coming to Me,
no need to stress or hurry
No need to state my case to the human race,
or the peanut gallery's judge and jury
No need to dig down deep in the ground,
or climb high up in a tree
I just keep vibing the vibe that brings me alive
and it ALL just comes to ME.

~dfc

I Can Feel Good Right Now

BLISSIPLINE- an unwavering determination to focus only on that which feels good.

If ever you feel to criticize

Just stop

And let

Your own dreams rise

~dr fun collective

The Awareness
of Lack and
of Appreciation
cannot both share
the stage
of our Attention

In each moment
we get to choose
which one
gets the spotlight
and which one
we cast in the leading role.

~dfc

I Can Feel Good Right Now

I am a thermostat. I SET the vibrational temperature of my experience.

~dFc

Read the following with all your heart and speak with deep conviction:

I, [your name] write my story.
I, __ write my book.
I, __ give meaning to my world.
I, __ bring my energy into every encounter in my experience.
I, __ decide what I want from life.
I, __ dream my adventures.
I, __ expand my awareness into new realms.
I, __ focus my attention on things that are pleasing to me.
I, __ spend my time doing what is the most fun for me.
I, __ share my joy with everyone in my path.
I, __ love myself with the love of a thousand oceans.
I, __ follow the impulses I am always receiving from my expanded self.
I, __ decide who I am, what I do, and why I'm here...

.... continue to rampage about your brilliant magnificence, your 24/7 access to the consciousness that creates worlds. Your complete control over your reality.
Right now.
Right now.
Right now!

~dFc

I Can Feel Good Right Now

The flow
The vibe
the wave
the ride
through Galaxies Dimensions
Black holes and white light
From end to end and side to side
It all boils down
To the FEELING inside.

~dfc

Unfolding, unfolding
Life's clay always molding
The best feeling thoughts
In each moment beholding.
~dFC

I Can Feel Good Right Now

We receive what we believe
and get what we emit,
so we can leave the other people out of it!

Energy-Lifter

It feels good to accept that I get MORE of what I FOCUS on.
It feels good to accept that I am PURE POSITIVE energy.
It feels good to accept that there are NO mistakes.
It feels good to accept that ALL IS WELL.
It feels good to accept that every new moment is PREGNANT with POSSIBILITY.
It feels good to accept that I am EXACTLY where I need to be.

It feels good to accept that I ATTRACT what I VIBRATE.
It feels good to accept that everything is perfect exactly as it is.
It feels good to accept that I've been here before and I'll be here again.
It feels good to accept that I chose to come here for the JOY of it.

It feels good to accept that I am TOTALLY AWESOME!
It feels good to accept that I am PERFECT exactly as I am.

I Can Feel Good Right Now

It feels good to accept that if I WANT it, I can HAVE it!

It feels good to accept that life is only getting BETTER for me.

It feels good to accept that I can best help others by my HAPPY example.

It feels good to accept that NO ONE needs my help.

It feels good to accept that being SELFISH is a good thing.

It feels good to accept that I am AMAZING!

It feels good to accept that all I have to do is RELAX and ALLOW and everything I desire will find it's way to me at the PERFECT time and in the PERFECT way.

It feels good to accept that I can BREATHE easy... Source has my back.

It feels good to accept that there will ALWAYS be something more to want.

It feels good to accept that I can dance if I want to and I can leave my friends behind, if my friends don't dance, cause if they don't dance, then they ain't no friends if mine.

Easier and easier
More and more fun
That's how I like
To get things done!!!

~dfc

I Can Feel Good Right Now

What are you doing Tim?
Well, I'm tuning and tuning
my vibrational dial
Until I come across a station
that makes me smile
Then I crank up the volume
and start bumpin' the bass
Until everyone in town
Can see the smile on my face

~dfc

Mind

The voice in your head is NOT leading you towards freedom.

It is there to keep you in line and coloring inside the lines.

The voice of freedom is soft and gentle and comes from the core of your being.

It doesn't run around your mind like your mother minutes before the dinner guests are due to arrive.

This is why quieting the mind is so central to receiving divine guidance.

~drfuncollective

What is the role of the brain
and our experience in receiving guidance from Source?
(A brief overview)

Each time we have an experience, our brain records it and keeps it accessible until the next time we encounter a similar situation.

On a practical level, this enables us to live more efficiently and effectively in our day to day lives. We know where the toilet is, we remember how to do basic tasks, we remember people's names and even certain attributes of their personality....this is ability is helpful in so many ways.

> But when it comes to the more mysterious, even unknown aspects of life, the brain can be less than helpful, even a hindrance!

Since the brain bases everything on what we've already experienced, it can only chart the future on the basis of the past. But what if we desire a future that differs from our past?

Instead of being an asset, the brain can be a hindrance. Our guidance from Source has direct access to our higher self, which is the part of us that knows all and sees all, and knows the best course of action to take us from where we are to where we desire to go. But this is very different than using the input of the brain. So, when it comes to staying open to the leading and guidance from our higher self, the brain has no point of reference, and is a rather ineffective resource.

Because most of us have been taught to use the brain as the best and final source of knowledge, this way of accessing guidance takes considerable practice.

I've been very conscious recently about how quieting the mind opens me up to never before experienced ways of living. Although it may feel comfortable to lean on my previous ways of doing and being, the newness of life can only come when I open myself up to the leading that comes from beyond the confines of my mind.

On a practical level, I often pause to breathe and quiet my mind. This is my way of acknowledging that it's not my job to mentally figure things out, but to stay in the receptive mode and use my focus on things that feel good.

This way, Source is free to do it's thaanggg!!

~dfc

I Can Feel Good Right Now

breathe in.
breathe out.
release,
relax,
it's all worked out!

~dfc

Quiet
the voices
to hear
the Voice

~dFc

I Can Feel Good Right Now

diving.
deep.
into this now
the voices swirling above
melt into murmurs and fade away
I.
am
alone now
with eternity

~dfc

I take a breath
I let it go
I still my mind
Now Source can flow

~dFc

I Can Feel Good Right Now

Whenever I feel rushed
or like I'm running short on time
I put on the brakes
and slow down
breathe deep
relax
realign

~dfc

I pause briefly
to breathe deeply
relaxing completely
I'm free to just be me.

~dfc

I Can Feel Good Right Now

I breathe in slowly
intentionally deep
resting still
feeling sure
all is well
I am complete

~dfc

A quiet mind invites magic

~dfc

I Can Feel Good Right Now

Consistently find the feeling behind what you desire and a matching collection of thoughts will begin to gather and make their home in your heart.

Stable eyes
Stabilized
Focused gaze
On bright blue skies
Becoming self
One breath away
Eternal bliss
Starts here today
~dFc

I Can Feel Good Right Now

It's your world. You make the rules and write the stories.

~dFc

The Story of it all

From our vibrational playground,

we chose to focus a SMALL PART of our infinite being-ness

HERE.

Planet Earth.

Why?

Expansion.

Expansion of the collection of vibrational energy that is "US"

For the Expansion of ALL that IS.

The mantra of the Universe is MORE.

This MORE comes through our Expansion.

My Expansion. Your Expansion. Our Expansion.

We EXPAND through CONTRAST

Through the SIFTING and SORTING.

In non-physical the contrast is more easily managed, less extreme, so..

We enter time and space.

Small

Helpless

Fleshy

Bundles of gummy, delightful smiles

and ear-piercing wails

food sucking, peeing, pooping bundles of

ME ME ME

I Can Feel Good Right Now

Our spirit continues to beam our eternal knowingness

But -

our mind has forgotten.

This was necessary in order for the contrast to have its way

The forgetting allows the contrast to surprise us

To shock us

To pain us

At times to crush us

But each time it happens

our spirit shoots a rocket

The rocket of preferred desire

Each rocket lands inside the greater part of us

Expansion has occurred

And it will continue to occur countless times during this orbital visit

The scale and scope of the CONTRAST

Is unique for each of us

Divinely guided from the director's chair of our GREATER KNOWING

Following the path of our unique trajectory.

An eternal trajectory

Recognized by its THEMES and TOPICS

that ENLIVENMENT and the INTRIGUE....

166 ~ Dr Fun

REPELLING and INFURIATING
its DEPTHS and INTENSITIES
the FEELINGS and the FLOWINGS
It's all GUIDANCE from our Higher Beingness

But even HERE, our natural state remains
BLISS and JOY
This is why contrast hurts.
Our joyful state has been momentarily
thwarted by a "problem"
We instantly become that baby again
We want our MOMMY
We want to eat NOW
We want to be held NOW
We want to play NOW

You see,
When our physical selves shoot these ROCKETS of DESIRE
Our higher self takes them and EXPANDS immediately
into previously UNKNOWN states of joy, love and awareness
We have just become MORE.
MORE. MORE. MORE than EVER BEFORE
in the history of the UNIVERSES...
EVER. EVER. EVER.
We become a new and expanded being as each rocket lands.

I Can Feel Good Right Now

If we follow quickly
We share this joy with our expanded selves
If we don't
It hurts
We have just SPLIT from ourselves.

It's at this point that our physical self,
in a desperate attempt to UNDERSTAND,
begins to tell stories
EPIC stories
Stories about the WORLD
Stories of pain and redemption
Stories of love lost and lessons learned
Stories of scarcity, lack, war, and heroes
Stories about US
Stories about THEM
About habits, and proclivities
Worthiness, guilt and shame
Superiority and inferiority
of helping and changing
of rage and revenge
Trying to make sense of it all.
The stories we create superficially satisfy our mind.

But our inner knowing is still speaking and guiding
telling the story of our eternal knowing

Gently prodding us to follow the expansion

to join our higher self on the magnificent ride of "moreness"

By finding any way possible

to unite with our higher selves in the place of expansion, bliss and joy.

Sing, dance, play, relax, be, allow, love, walk, sleep, eat....

Find anyway to

Feel Good. Feel Joy. Feel Freedom. Have Fun.

Will we align with our true nature of JOY, BLISS, FUN

while we are still HERE

and begin living from the new places of joy

that we have created?

OR

Will we habitually resist and focus on what "went wrong"

On what we need to change in ourselves and others

Pushing, probing, ranting, fixing and staying...

to some degree, disconnected?

The GOOD NEWS is

that in the end

either way

We will all RECEIVE and BECOME

the EXPANDED SELVES that we have created.

I Can Feel Good Right Now

The only question really, is.

Will we resist until the day we croak

holding ourselves apart from the expansion that we've created?

OR

Will we find ways to align here and now?

And feel our new joyful expansion

Moment by Moment

Day by Day

And start our lives of "happily ever after" today?

Either way, when we croak

we'll become the fullness of the expansion that we've created

It comes down to how much fun we decide to have along the way.

~dr Fun collective

Find ANY reason you can to
FEEL GOOD NOW!

~dFc

About the Author

Tim McGinnis

I am Dr Fun. I'm passionate about communicating leading-edge universal truths through music, word and dramatic presentation, to help people understand themselves better and live happier lives.

My passion to understand myself and my place in the world has been a long and complex process. Answers have not come easily to me, but what has come, is an acute ability to understand the underlying principles of life and happiness and with it, an earnest desire to communicate what I am learning to anyone curious enough to want to understand. I use short and catchy songs to help people feel better, by shaping their moment by moment thoughts in order to harness the power of their focus.

I am continually asking questions, receiving answers and finding creative and revolutionary ways to communicate these truths. I love bringing ideas that typically stay under the surface of everyday consciousness and emerge into the forefront of life's experiences in a happy and easy manner.

Published

Mill House publishers,
Mill House, Møllehavevej 11
3200 Helsinge
Denmark
T: +45 87959911
www.millhouse-publishers.com